# One Summer

Jeffrey WILLIAMS
Illustrated by Kylie Baker

*This book is dedicated to My Mom, she always taught me to do my best and be the best I could be. Through her sickness sometimes I would write day and night. She would still say to me. Anything you put your mind to, you can do it. And I never gave up.*

I would like to extend my appreciation to Celia Kerr. She inspired and encouraged me to believe that I had a pathway to walk on in this journey of writing. A special thank you to Dr. Kimberly P. Johnson. I went to her thinking that I had it all figured out. She said, "I will help you, but don't waste my time - you have to be serious about writing." She taught me the true meaning of writing and how to fill in all of my holes. She taught me that writing was more than words, its about feelings too. And I can't thank her enough. To Micheal Kinion for some odd reason when I looked at this guy, I thought - I'm not gonna like him. But I mentioned a book that I was writing to him and I told him that I wasn't satisfied with the graphic artist. He recommended Kylie Baker. She became my illustrator... and now hopefully everyone will enjoy the great artwork throughout the book. She made the story breathe with her heartfelt visuals. Gloria Dixon, Rose McElhaney, Nyetta Cloud, Kimberly Givens, Meika Jones and Melissa Thomas, I say thanks again. I am sure that I have probably missed someone, I thank you for what you taught me. Every interaction in my life has brought about a story. Zoe Ranucci, came along just in time to put the finishing touches and render a fantastic layout. Not just to do a service, but to go over and beyond to create a great first book.

Last but by no means least... my amazing wife and kids. They were my backbone and I remember when I first heard their words, "Dad you still working on your book?" that was enough to let me know that I was in it to win it.

For information address the author at ridendark@gmail.com

Edited By Simply Creative™ Works

Illustration by Kylie Baker

Design by Zoe Ranucci, www.gooddharma.com

ISBN: 978-1-5136-8553-3

U

# Contents

# Prologue

Finally, the school days were almost over!! You could see the excitement and energy of the teachers as they packed up their memories from the year.  From drawings to puzzles to Lego shaped creatures, everything would be piled into large containers until the next school year. On top of that, everyone was becoming more and more restless as the summer days crept closer. Kids were sitting around the cafeteria talking about upcoming summer plans and trying to figure out what would be the coolest thing to do over the summer. Each year had to be better than the one before...

# A Challenging Year

# CHAPTER 1

"Well it's almost here-thank God!!", exclaimed Lamar, "The day can't come soon enough!"

"It hasn't been THAT bad", chimed Ally. "Have you lost your mind? This has been the worst year of my life, especially since I barely passed math", echoed Caleb, "I swear that teacher was out to get me with trapezoids and cumulative properties! The good thing is that it's over, we have a ton of things to look forward to this summer...let's talk about that!"

"I agree", replied Lamar. They all leaned their heads in together at the table as if they were strategically planning to create a secret invention or some type of magical potion. There were just a few days left until the school door would close and the summer session of fun, laughter, sleeping in, and fishing would officially begin. Just as they were getting deep into the planning – the bell rang and reminded them that their plans weren't quite ready to be launched – it was time to head back to class and …classwork! The good thing was that today was

Friday and nothing could stop Saturday from being a great day to finish their planning.

The next day everyone gathered by the local lake to finish the master planning. “Hey, where is Ally?” asked Lamar. “Well, yesterday she wasn’t that happy about her grades”,

Caleb replied, "Let's just hope that she'll get here soon!" The kids loved spending time together but never knew time as numbers. Everything was determined by the sun. The sun was their clock and it was always the best way to tell what needed to be done. But before they could really get into the depth of their planning, the sun backed up into the clouds and the ground was no longer bright and sunny.

While they sat laughing on the ground, waiting for Ally, the clouds began to cover the sun. Drops of rain quickly started to fall. Lamar blurted out, "Oh no, plans destroyed, run to the trees for cover." They all jumped up and raced toward the enormous oak tree that was their favorite climbing spot, but today it was all about shielding themselves from the heavy drops of rain.

They waited under the trees to hear the best ideas. Ally had finally showed up, but she was drenched from the heavy rain and was focusing more on drying her ponytails. Caleb spoke up, "I've got an idea!" Caleb was always late to show up, but always seemed to have the best ideas. "The gym at the children's home is always empty. Maybe, if we offer to help them, they will let us use the gym and play there when we have days like this. In the summer, the huge gym was a vacant building that just sat there unused. Lamar blurted out, “What a great idea. I love basketball and I never thought of that!” They all grinned - Caleb was always thinking of things they never thought of – he was always thinking.

The children’s home would be a great place to hang out and have some summer fun when the time arrived. The children’s home was a learning gym that would help kids with disabilities. Caleb’s brother, Greyson, happened to be one of the kids who loved the gym. Greyson was autistic and liked hanging with Caleb and his friends. They added him to their group as an honorary member. In the summertime, the children from the home usually went to visit their families or on special vacations. Caleb was lucky enough to spend his whole summer with Greyson. In fact, Greyson would go with them to the children’s home to hang out in the gym. Caleb’s mom, Mrs. Wilson, had volunteered at the home since Greyson was born and knew the director well. She could help them convince the director to let them use the gym a couple of days a week. Mrs. Wilson was a nice lady and Caleb always talked about how much she loved volunteering at the children’s home. She started volunteering there right after the family found out that Greyson had Autism. They helped her realize that Greyson could do a lot of things and that he had a lot of opportunities to be successful. In fact, Greyson was rather good at basketball and could make some long shots. Maybe, she could help them convince the director to let them use the gym a couple of days a week. They loved Greyson at the gym, which meant that they might love Caleb and his friends too. Caleb was going to get busy working on that.

In the meantime, the kids needed to focus on their final tests for the year. Landon hated taking tests, but he knew that he had a great year and could possibly do well on his final grades. A week later, everyone had passed their final tests and the school year had finally ended. Caleb's mom had worked a miracle and convinced the director to let them use the gym under one condition: they had to come in every Saturday morning and help with extra cleaning and yard work.

# 2

# The Happy Trapper

# CHAPTER 2

When the first day of summer break started the kids agreed to meet at the gym. Everyone arrived at different times – filed into the gym – and began practice. Before long, the gym was filled with the melodies of bouncing basketballs. Greyson was off to the side bouncing a basketball …all by himself. Landon wandered over to Greyson, "Hey maybe you'd like a friend to play with." Before long, Greyson and Landon were in a dribble competition and they were both laughing and hustling the ball back and forth. Greyson started rushing so hard toward the ball that he accidentally kicked it with great force. The ball bounced a few times and headed toward the open gym door. "Hold up Greyson, I'll get it", Landon raced toward the gym door and the ball spun through the door onto the grass and down a hill. Landon looked back and realized that Greyson was right behind him. Landon chuckled to himself and shook his head. The ball rolled and landed right in front of a barbed wire fence. That is when Greyson noticed a woman carrying a large bucket of water. Greyson shouted, "That's Mrs. Martha, she's going to feed her chickens and give them water!!".

You could see her struggling as she hauled the large bucket. Water splashed back and forth in and out of the bucket. Landon yelled, “Hey could you use a hand with that?”

Mrs. Martha flung the bucket down and put her hands on her hips. She squinted to see who had shouted at her. “Do I know you young man?” “Hey Mrs. Martha, it’s me,

- Greyson." "Oh Greyson, what are you doing here this summer?", she asked. She walked toward the fence wiping sweat from her forehead. "I am here with my brother, and this is my friend Landon", said Greyson. Landon smiled at Mrs. Martha and once again offered to help with the bucket of water. "I sure could use the help", she admitted. Landon walked down toward the hinged gate and flipped the lock. Again, Greyson was on his heels. Landon hoisted up the bucket and followed Mrs. Martha to the barn.

After they fed and watered the chickens, she thanked the young men for their help and invited them back anytime. Greyson and Landon raced back through the fence and grabbed the ball. As they headed up the hill toward the gym Caleb came down to meet them. "Where did you guys go? We're done for the day!" Landon turned and pointed down the hill to Mrs. Martha's farm, "there" he stated, "to help". Caleb said, "yea, she's nice." "Come on Greyson, we've got to get home", replied Caleb. The boys waved goodbye and headed their separate ways.

Landon decided to take the route by the lake today, he wanted to be outside a little longer for some reason. Landon was definitely a country boy – he loved being outdoors and being with nature. There was no greater joy than when he could climb trees and steep hills, or race through the woods. He especially loved the narrow dirt path that led to the Creekside. He always found it to be a quiet space that allowed him to think about life and all of the other things in the world. Landon was a deep thinker and thinking helped him focus on the things he needed to do.

Landon strolled down the path and found a rock that caught his attention. He decided to engage in a light game of kick the rock. As Landon kicked the rock down the narrow path, he noticed tiny footprints along the edge of the creek – did something come up out of the water to the edge of the creek, he thought to himself. He felt a tinge of excitement – what could it have been? Why was it there? How could he catch this interesting creature?

Landon immediately raced home to grab his trapping cage. He knew that it would be a long shot to catch anything without anything to lure it so he reached inside of his supply bag and pulled out a can of meat. Could he possibly find a wild animal that he could tame? The idea of doing that made Landon even more excited. But he had to be patient. Patience was the secret to being good at trapping and Landon knew that. He headed

back home and wished the night away, because morning would and could possibly bring him his dream – raising a wild creature.

To Landon, trapping and taming was only a game. He could not wait for the sun to rise, he wondered "who would win?" Finally, daybreak arrived, and Landon raced through the secret paths, he could feel his heart beat faster and faster as he hurried through the brush. When he arrived at the hilltop, he gasped. There before him along the creek sat the downward cage. Landon cried out, "I trapped it!" With a closer look, he spotted the footprints of where the animal had walked around. When he approached the cage – he was surprised…NOTHING!! There was nothing in the cage! The animal had taken the bait and left!!Landon was shocked and hurt at the same time. He felt deep down that the animal would be back for another chance at free food, but right now Landon was feeling the defeat of the moment. He grabbed another can of the bait from inside his shoulder bag, same scent and same size – he would place it back into the cage and wait...patiently for the creature to return. This time he wouldn't get away so easily!

Landon tried to sleep that night, but his mind was on the cage and trapping the creature. He lay awake in bed excited about the feeling that he would have when daybreak came. He tried to think about how proud he would be to share the news with his friends. As he laid in bed imagining the feeling, sleep crept upon him and stole his thoughts.

# 3

# The Special Horse

# CHAPTER 3

The next day, Landon bounced out of bed and jumped into his clothes. He raced out of the door barely closing it and rushed into the woods. He ran as fast as he could down the same route. He felt his heart beating faster and faster. Landon could hear the animal as it rattled around in the trap. Landon could hear the quickness of the creature's paw pacing back and forth. He knew that this time he had caught something for sure. He could only imagine the types of creatures that could have found their way into the cage – as he rounded the corner… there it was…

**a racoon**!

The wild strength of the animal began to fade inside the cage, as Landon approached the cage from the other side. He saw the racoon begin to frantically paw and bite and growl in its cage. Landon tried to calm the wild animal but there was no use – it was determined to get out of the cage. He picked the cage up and wrestled with it for a few minutes before the raccoon calmed down. Finally, the wrestling of the cage stopped – Landon had won!! The raccoon finally sat in the corner of the cage and waited for the final destination. Landon hauled the cage back through the woods to his house. He felt like the happiest kid ever because he had finally become a trapper. Plans started rushing through his head on how he would tame the wild animal. He couldn't wait to share those thoughts with the other kids at the children's home. They would be so proud of him and his fearlessness!

The heavy drops of rain began to roll from the sky. Landon had gotten caught in the downpour only to find out that the gym door at the children's home was locked. You could tell that the racoon was more bothered about being trapped in the cage than the torrential downpour of rain. Landon couldn't believe that the gym was closed over a little rain – For him rain was never an enemy …he welcomed the relaxing sounds and feelings.

As the weight of the cage increased, Landon looked at the scared raccoon and began to think about what he had done. He reflected on how he had taken the freedom from this wild animal. He realized that some animals are meant to be free in the wild and not trapped as human pets. Landon made the mistake of catching a glimpse of the racoon's eyes and he felt that he somehow had betrayed a trusted friend. For the first time Landon didn't think that trapping helpless animals was so cool after-all. And suddenly he realized that standing in a downpour wasn't too smart either as the troubling winds picked up and thunder began to approach – Landon raced towards Mrs. Martha's barn – doing everything he could to protect the helpless racoon.

"Come on in here", yelled Mrs. Martha. "Who in the world would be roaming around in this weather with an animal cage?!" Landon set the cage down and looked out of the barn just in time to see the crack of lightning ripple across the sky. The horses were frightened by the thunderous sound and began to gather around the old wooden barn. Landon couldn't believe how many horses gathered around the open doors almost as if they were hoping for permission to come in out of the horrendous weather. Landon peeped out of the side window in the barn and spotted one horse standing under a drooping willow tree. Landon shouted to Mrs. Martha, "Come quick, there's one horse still way out there under the willow tree, we need to get him closer to the barn." Mrs. Martha knew instantly that Landon was referring to Magic – the wild spotted

stallion. Mrs. Martha shook her head and responded – "I watch this horse stay far out in the field from day to day. He seems to be happier out there than close to this old wooden barn. I usually try to let him be until it's time to have him shoed or for a vet visit. He seems to enjoy being alone out there free and with nature. The willow tree is his home".

Mrs. Martha's thoughts drifted off, "he's the most beautiful horse that I've ever seen, and he needs the most patience. Perhaps if one day you can learn to tame him .... he's yours!" Landon's eyes quickly shifted to Mrs. Martha. Was she serious? Was this indeed a challenge?

# 4 Best Direction

# CHAPTER 4

Landon looked down at the trapped raccoon and realized that no animal should ever feel trapped. Maybe Magic felt trapped when he was inside the barn and closed in by the other animals. He needed his freedom and so did this raccoon. The rain slowed down and Landon hoisted the cage up and asked Mrs. Martha if he could set the racoon free at the edge of her woods. Mrs. Martha replied, "I think that is probably a good idea – every animal deserves to be free – especially if they want to be". Landon shook his head in agreement and looked out at Magic once again. You're right, he said, every animal deserves to know the taste of freedom – especially the wild ones – especially the wild ones."

All the way home Landon thought about the special horse. "All he needs is a friend," he whispered to himself. Landon remembered the times when he went places and his friends didn't want to hang with him. Sometimes they had a good reason for not wanting to include him, but most of the time they didn't have a good reason at all. He knew how that

felt and he couldn't imagine how Magic must feel standing all alone under that Willow Tree. Landon was determined to do what he could to help him feel important and special. Every creature needs to know that they are loved, and he was determined to show Magic that he was loved too.

The next morning when Landon arrived at the barn he was greeted by Greyson. Greyson liked to spend time with Mrs. Martha just to get away from his brothers and sometimes just to see the animals that roamed in and out of the barnyard. Greyson raced over to the fence, "Hey what are you doing here Landon?" "I came to see my new friend Magic", Landon replied. "He doesn't like new people", chimed Greyson, "He's a loner". Greyson was probably right because the closer Landon got to Magic the farther Magic moved onto the open area of the field. Landon was starting to feel heartbroken that Magic wanted nothing to do with him. "It's okay Landon, it took him a long time to like me too. At first, I thought he just didn't like people with autism but then I realized that he doesn't like that many people at all. Plus, he's wild and wild horses don't like people that much" Greyson snickered. "Besides, he's just a special horse…don't give up! He likes treats though."

Then Landon got a great idea; perhaps he could lure him closer with the piece of peppermint that he had wedged in the corner of his jacket pocket. He could not stand peppermints but every time he went to visit his grandmother, she insisted that he stick one in his pocket and he happened to have one tucked in the corner of his jacket. This would be an excellent treat to get the relationship started. Greyson peeped around the back of Landon to see what he was digging out of his pocket - "yay he likes peppermints, but he would like apples better" said Greyson. Landon smiled and nodded his head he knew just the spot to get huge, juicy apples, but the trick was would *SHE* help? The "*SHE*" was Mrs. Rose, the elderly lady on the corner of street in Landon's neighborhood. She loved flowers but everyone thought she hated kids. It's kind of ironic that her name was Mrs. *Rose* when she was more like a cactus – always ready to prick at anyone who crossed her – especially if they were on her property – at least that was what the rumors were.

"Mom" Landon reported, "I need apples for my new friend Magic". "Sure, fruit is healthy for the body and I am glad that you are starting to eat more of it, tell your friend Magic I said thanks" Mom replied. Landon laughed out loud and said,

"Mom, he's my new best friend, but he's a horse!" "Well

that's not a nice thing to say about him." "No Mom, for real… he's a horse", Landon exclaimed. "So, you want me to start buying fruit for a horse?" she inquired. "No – we can get it from Mrs. Rose's tree if only we can do it at the right time". Mom shook her head, "I'm not sure if there is ever a right time for Mrs. Rose". Landon suggested, "Perhaps we can work as a team – maybe you can visit her and then I can snag a few of the apples, while you guys are talking."

"Do you mean steal them?" mom echoed with a frown. "Instead of stealing, let's try to talk to her and get her in a good mood. After that Landon you can come in and ask her to let you grab some of the apples off the ground. But you have to promise her that you'll walk carefully around her flowers. She loves her flower beds", Mom replied. "Thanks, Mom I didn't think of that – I just thought of grabbing and running." They both laughed and headed towards Mrs. Rose's house.

"Let's take the ATV", Mom suggested, "and we can take the shortcut." Landon jumped on the back of the ATV and his Mom reminded, "Remember your helmet and seat belt. Let's go!".

Landon had to have the coolest mom in the neighborhood. She wasn't afraid of anything...the dark, the woods or even wild animals. She was supportive of anything that made Landon happy…as long as it was the right thing to do! When they approached Mrs. Rose's …her porch light had just gone dark. "Oh, no…..she won't open the door I bet. Let's try", Mom suggested. Once they rang the doorbell, Mrs. Rose said in a sweet voice, "Come on in". Landon and his mom looked at each other, this wasn't the *cactus* that they had heard about.

# 5

# The Surprise

# CHAPTER 5

They opened the wooden door that was dressed in colorful flowers – and immediately spotted the welcome mat which would normally be on the outside. '*That's odd*', thought Landon. "Hello Mrs. Rose, sorry to bother you so late in the evening", said Mom. "No problem, I was about to lay down, but how can I help you?" "I'm not sure if you remember me but I am Alice Reid and this is my son Landon." "I can't say that I know you – and how did you say you know me?" Mrs. Rose asked. Landon quickly held his head down as Mom gave him the evil eye. He would dare not tell her that the kids at school called her the *Cactus lady*!

"Well Mrs. Rose, you are known throughout the community for your beautiful flowers and you certainly are the talk of the town." Mrs. Rose blushed as she flipped her wrist toward Alice and Landon. "Oh, do tell, they're just what I need to keep me living. There is nothing like digging around in the soil and playing with them. I truly consider them my children. Believe it or not, Rose is really my nickname – I've been called that since I was a child because I always took a Rose for show and tell – they are truly my favorite flowers. But I am sure you didn't stop by tonight to talk about flowers, so how can I help you?" "My son Landon has fallen in love with a horse named Magic and he needs some apples to take to him." Mrs. Rose smirked and nodded her head, "Well, he looks old enough to ask for himself." Landon looked up almost embarrassed by Mrs. Rose's comment – "Yes ma'am, you're right – I apologize it just slipped my mind."

"I don't mind giving you a donation to feed your horse but you need to ask me for what you want." "Well I don't really need a donation; I only need apples from your apple tree beyond the flower bed. Mrs. Rose leaned her head to the side, "What apple tree are you referring to, son?" Landon replied, "The bright colored tree at the edge of the yard, it's full of apples and that is all my horse needs". Mrs. Rose broke out into a hearty laugh, she laughed so hard that Landon and his Mom started laughing with her. Landon grabbed his stomach and said, "What are we all laughing about?" Mrs. Rose wiped the tears from her eyes and said, "With my eyesight so bad, I just thought that was a bright tree full of red leaves and I didn't realize the leaves were actually apples. I just never walked out that far to see for myself!" They all started laughing again and realized that Mrs. Rose had a great sense of humor and was really a nice lady after all.

Mrs. Rose said, "Son what's your name again, sometimes age just gets the best of me and I've been all alone since moving from another country". "My name is Landon", he replied, "Wow where did you move from?". Alice, snapped, "Landon that is rude, you are being invasive, maybe she just likes being alone." "Mrs. Rose responded, "No worries, I'm from Thailand." "I've heard of Thailand before – that's a long way away. So how did you get here?" Landon inquired. "When my husband was alive, we loved visiting America because this was his favorite place to visit. He loved going to the beaches, fishing, and visiting the amusement parks. He loved a good roller coaster ride! And so, did I!" Landon's eyes grew wide. He just couldn't see Mrs. Rose on a roller coaster. "After he died, I didn't want to have so many memories, so I moved away and came to the place that we loved." "Mrs. Rose, what a beautiful story", smiled Alice. A true love match – Landon felt like hugging Mrs. Rose but was afraid that she wouldn't know how to accept a hug since she seemed so comfortable being alone.

"Enough of that, let's get back to Maggie" – both Alice and Landon looked at each other and said – "Who's Maggie?" "What is the horse's name again?" asked Mrs. Rose, "It's Magic," Landon replied. "Oh, that's right – I told you age has a way of getting the best of me!" Mrs. Rose grinned. "Yes, back to the beautiful apple tree. Landon take all you need – all I ask is that you walk in the paths, so you don't accidentally step on my flowers. I treat them like my life, they're all I have to take care of!"

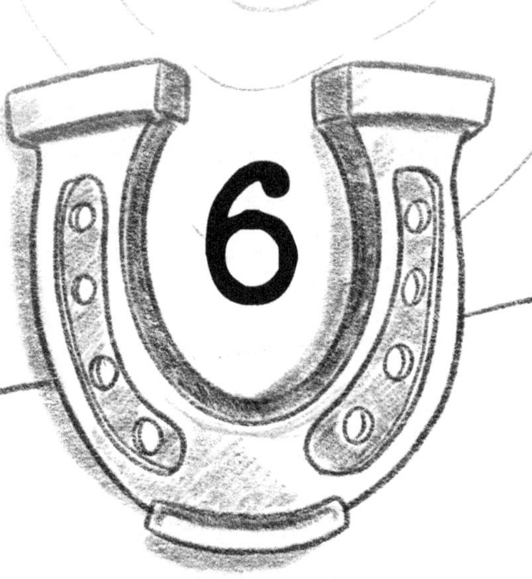


# The Beginning of the Bond

# CHAPTER 6

Everyday Landon's mission was to get closer to Magic. He was excited about starting to get the apples. Landon knew that the fresh scent from the apples would attract Magic and make their bond even stronger. Landon believed that the taste of the apples would be one that Magic would look forward to and never forget. He was grateful that Mrs. Rose had agreed to help. Landon was also glad that the apple treats would never run out! Landon had to wait a little while until the apples were just right for picking. He went by each day to check on the Summer Rambo apples. Landon had been studying the kind of apples that filled Mrs. Rose's tree. Each time Landon went by to check on the apples, he shared more information with her about the apples AND about Magic.

Landon got to know Mrs. Rose a little more and more. Finally, Landon felt comfortable enough with Mrs. Rose and took a chance and hugged her... she hugged him back. He could feel her kindness as she wrapped her arms around him. Landon could only imagine how her flowers must have felt with this kind of love.

Mrs. Rose was not the mean, old lady that many of the kids had made her out to be. She was a kind and caring lady, who just needed to have friends. Landon was going to be her friend too, not just because she gave him apples, but just because he wanted to. He was excited that the summer had introduced him to not one, but two new friends!

Landon woke up the next morning and looked out his bedroom window. He noticed the clouds. This made him nervous because he knew that rain would soon follow and maybe even thunder too. He quickly threw back his covers and got ready. He grabbed his raincoat and headed to Mrs. Rose's yard to stuff his backpack with fresh, juicy apples. This would be the day that Magic would have his first treat from the tree. Magic was the only thing on his mind at that moment. He waved goodbye to Mrs. Rose and hurried toward Mrs. Martha's barn, but the mixture of wind and rain had already arrived. Landon felt the cold rain pound against his face. As he got closer to Magic, Magic started backing away. This was not what he wanted to happen. The surprise was supposed to bring them closer, not separate them. The wind picked up and Magic became more and more agitated with the weather and it even looked as if he was getting agitated with Landon. Landon knew the only hope was to let Magic see the treats. As he tried to get closer to Magic, his foot slipped on the wet grass and Landon hit the ground. *Thump!* Landon looked up and could only see the huge animal and his strong legs hovering over his crouched-up body.

The animal's legs seemed to be crawling on air – this was perhaps the scariest moment in Landon's life but at the same time it was an incredible picture to see this huge animal from a different angle.

Landon had to think quickly. He reached into his bag and pulled the apples out and tossed them across the ground in a different direction. Suddenly, Magic turned and began to prance around and around. This had certainly gotten his attention. Magic had shown fancy footwork in just a few seconds. That same fancy footwork could have crushed Landon within seconds!! Luckily, Mrs. Rose's apples had perhaps saved Landon's life.

Magic ran off and looked down at the apples, then he glanced over at Landon as if to say– "*I could have hurt you if I wanted to, but I chose not to*". Perhaps this was the moment that Landon and Magic would remember forever. Magic had proven that he had a huge heart and that he would never intentionally hurt Landon. Even though at that moment, Landon couldn't help but flash back on the thought of the huge beast lunging over him. He had never felt so scared in his life! Landon had done nothing to Magic but try to be nice. Why would this animal set out to harm Landon or anyone else? Had he been hurt in the past and this triggered a memory for Magic? Was he just showing off his massive strength? Why had he reacted in this way? If only Landon could ask him "*Why? Why did he choose not to hurt him*? It certainly wasn't just the apples... Magic had plenty of time to do harm, but he didn't… *he didn't.*

When Landon got home, he couldn't help but to think how lucky he was that he had not been trampled by this huge beast. He wanted to tell his mom and dad what had happened, but he was afraid that they would never let him return, so he kept the secret to himself. Perhaps he was crazy to even want to go back to that place. However, something deep inside of him made him anxious and excited to see Magic again. Even though it was a scary moment, Landon couldn't wait for daylight – he would return to the stable and this time he wouldn't take anything. He would return empty handed. Would Magic treat him differently – if he didn't come bringing gifts? Landon needed to know that Magic would be his friend, no matter what. He needed to build that kind of relationship with Magic and he was determined to make that happen. He pulled off the water drenched clothes from the day and threw them into the laundry basket, grabbed a quick bite and headed toward his computer. He needed to relax his mind from the day. Tomorrow would be a challenging day, perhaps the toughest day of the summer! He would start trying to train Magic.

# Just a Little More Time

# CHAPTER 7

Daylight peeked through the window and Landon woke to the familiar smell of breakfast but even that could not distract him from getting to the stable to start his day with Magic. He jumped out of bed and immediately washed up and brushed his teeth. This morning, he decided to skip breakfast and he raced out of the door – turning quickly to yell. "See you later Mom". Before Landon's Mom could say a word, Landon had grabbed his bicycle, which was propped up against the side of the house and pedaled as fast as he could to Mrs. Martha's barn.

When he arrived, he heard a sound and he knew it was Magic but was Magic saying hello or was he preparing himself for a new conquest. Landon's main goal today was to get closer to Magic, without an attack. As Landon looked across the grassy field – he could see Magic running around and around. Mrs. Martha came out of her house and waved to Landon. She admitted, "Magic seems to be acting a bit odd today – not sure what is going on. Maybe he was waiting for you to arrive." Landon, cocked his head in amazement – "Do you think, he is waiting for me?" Mrs. Martha shook her head, "I think so". At that moment Landon raced across the field screaming Magic's name all the way. At that moment, Magic began to move toward Landon. Suddenly, Magic stopped. This caused Landon to stop as well. The only thing Landon could think to do was to run back to get some apples. Landon also knew that if he kept giving him treat's he would never know if Magic really just liked *him*.

"*Maybe I'll just reach out my hand and see if that will be enough*", Landon thought to himself. He nervously raised his hand into the air and Magic lowered his head but still did not move. Magic only watched as Landon stood there with an empty hand. Landon decided that there were other chores that needed to be done- Magic was not cooperating. He decided that perhaps today wasn't the day to work with Magic. Landon would have to wait until another day to deal with Magic's insecurities. This disappointed Landon, but he had to be tough or Magic would never cooperate.

Landon turned to head back towards the barn, but then out of nowhere there was another sound from Magic – Landon looked over his shoulder and realized that Magic had taken a few more steps forward. Landon's heart began to race, but a few seconds later Magic paused and turned around to head towards the willow tree for a nap. Mrs. Martha spotted Landon coming in from the open field, “What happened? Don’t look so sad”. “He doesn’t want to have anything to do with me today”, Landon replied. Mrs. Martha put her hand on Landon’s shoulder, “Don’t worry, everything takes time. Believe it or not, there was a time that Magic always stood alone but now he gets excited to know that you are here”. “For real?” Landon echoed, “For real”, Mrs. Martha grinned. “Come back tomorrow and try again, he’ll warm up more to you... you’ll see”. Mrs. Martha’s confidence and encouragement gave Landon a degree of hope that he had not experienced before. Maybe he was going to be a great friend to Magic, maybe Magic just needed a little time to make friends.

As Landon walked up the hill toward the gym at the children’s home, Greyson came tearing down the hill yelling, “Hey Landon, Hey Friend”. Suddenly Landon felt inspired by Greyson, the great motivator. “Hey Landon, how are you with Magic your new horse friend?” Landon snickered at the name *horse friend.* “Pretty good I guess, he doesn’t seem to like me sometimes,” Landon admitted. “That’s okay I don’t like you sometimes either.” They both laughed and wandered into the gym to cool off. Greyson said, "I told you that patience teaches us the best way and dreams that seem farthest away are always closer to your heart". Landon looked at Greyson in amazement, at times it seemed that Greyson was much older than an 11-year old. So wise for his age.

Another day had passed and all of the kids from the children's home decided to meet in Mrs. Martha's office. Their job was to gather hay for the horses to have in the winter. As they loaded up on the wagon to head to the field, most of the

kids didn't even know what it meant to work this hard. They jumped off of the wagon and began to watch each other as they gathered the hay. Soon, the kids were laughing and hoisting hay upon the wagon. Hard work didn't seem to bother them, and Magic was the farthest thing from their minds. After a long day of hard work and laughter, Mrs. Martha ventured out towards the barn. She placed her arm on Landon's shoulder and said, "In all of my years of gathering hay – I have never seen Magic come this close to the barn – he must have heard your voice Landon". Landon looked up and smiled broadly at Mrs. Martha, "For Real?", he inquired. "For real" she assured. At that point Landon reached for a bottle of water from his backpack but instead an apple treat fell out. Landon reached down to grab the treat and when Landon looked up Magic was standing there ready for his treat. He hadn't seen Landon all day and it almost seemed as if he were anxious to re-visit his old friend. The hardest day of work had suddenly become the best day of Landon's life. This connection with Magic had changed everything.

# 8 Unwelcome Guest

# CHAPTER 8

From then on, Magic would always listen for Landon's whistle and as soon as he heard it, Magic let out loud sounds that assured Landon that he was on the way. It was their beautiful way of communicating with each other. Though it was obvious that they had grown closer, the goal was still to ride Magic and that had not been accomplished yet!

For Landon, training was still necessary to prevent dangerous situations from occurring. Landon grabbed a rope from the closet in the shed, he would lead Magic to the training pen. Mrs. Martha saw him grab the rope and yelled, "No, don't use a rope that will spook him! You must try another way to get him to the training pen. He was once abused by a previous owner." She added, "Closed spaces may not be safe to work with him." Landon needed to be able to get Magic to the old training area at the barn - that's where the real work would begin. However, Mrs. Martha had made the task even more difficult. "What happened to him?" Landon inquired. Mrs. Martha admitted, "It was horrible, he was beaten and almost starved to death. It turns out that a family bought him to use him as a show horse, but when they ran out of money – they no longer could take care of him, so they just left him and a rescue organization found him." "Why didn't they just give him to someone who could take care of him?" Landon asked. "Selfish people, I guess Landon…selfish people. Now it is hard for Magic to truly trust anyone. That is why I'm really surprised that he let you get close to him this fast." Landon started crying, "Oh my gosh, how could anyone do this? I wouldn't dare try to scare him like that." It took Landon about 20 minutes to gather himself, Magic just stood there patiently waiting for Landon to give him a sign of what to do next. Landon thought, "*Maybe he'll just follow me to the pen and get familiar with the area*." That would be Landon's strategy at least for now.

It was Landon and Magic every day until suddenly one of Mrs. Martha's roosters arrived to scrutinize the situation with Magic and Landon. The spotted rooster flew to the top post shouting out his loud crow. It felt strange but Landon wanted to ask him why he was there – but the rooster seemed to be comfortable sitting on his high post just watching the antics of both Magic and Landon. What was thought of as an easy task

turned into more of a challenging situation. Still no luck and another day almost gone. Suddenly, Landon remembered his parents told him that he had to get home before dark.

As he rode toward his house, he kept thinking how he was going to lure Magic into the training pen. When he arrived home he wandered into his bedroom and fell onto his bed. His mind kept spinning around, thinking about how cruel that family had been to Magic for no reason at all. He wondered how he was going to accomplish his task of gaining Magic's trust. Finally, sleep overcame him and he drifted into a deep slumber.

Landon rolled over and was met by the vibrant sun that shone through his window. The new day awakened him to the same thoughts…*how, how, how would he accomplish his task*? He bounced out of bed and rushed toward the bathroom to get ready. For some strange reason, he had more energy than he had ever experienced. Once he was dressed, he rushed to the kitchen for a quick breakfast snack. Magic was the only thing on his mind, he could think of a lot better things to do on a Thursday morning than spend the day at the barn. However, something about that horse kept drawing him there. Landon raced to his bike and headed through the path that landed him

a few feet from the barn. Landon let out a loud whistle, this was to alert Magic that he had arrived and would be expecting to see him.

You could hear Magic making his loud horse sound in response, as if to say, *I'm over here friend.* Landon ran to the training pen hoping that Magic would follow his voice. Soon after, Landon arrived at the training pen, he spun around to see Magic standing there stomping. Landon shouted, "It worked, my plan worked!!" Now if only he could get him to come inside of the pen he thought to himself, he could begin his training lessons.

Magic stood at the door of the training pen still hesitant about walking through. There the recycling tub filled with aluminum cans was just a few feet away. An enormous horse fly flew ahead – buzzing and swarming around Magic, trying his best to distract him. It was starting to irritate Magic. Sweeping his tail, Magic continuously missed as the horsefly waited for the point of attack. As the horsefly pierced Magic in the center of his back, Magic vigorously spun his neck around attempting to swipe the horsefly away – tipping the container of aluminum cans over – cans scattered everywhere around Magic's hooves. *Crunch, crunch* was all you could hear as Magic's powerful hooves obliterated the cans. Before Magic knew it he had lunged into the training pen.

# 9

# A Friend of a Beast

# CHAPTER 9

The thought of being inside the training pen spooked Magic beyond belief. Magic's ears peaked up and he rocked his head back and forth. Landon had been around horses enough to know that if he saw a horse's ears lay back, he knew that meant they were scared or uncomfortable. Landon could tell that the horse was looking for a way out but could not find the pen door. Magic felt trapped and now he was prepared to react to what he was feeling.  His front legs rose into the air and his back legs kicked out sideways. Landon had never seen anything like this before. It was as if Magic grew 10 more feet right there in front of him. From that he began to spin around and around. Landon had nowhere to go – he found himself pressed against the wall of the pen, his heart was about to beat out of his chest. He could see the pen door but had no idea how he would maneuver his way over to the latch.

Magic headed towards Landon and raised his front legs up high above Landon's head. Landon crouched down – too scared to even scream. He covered his head knowing that this could possibly be the last time he'd ever breathe again. Landon had a terrible flashback from the last time that he saw Magic's legs up in the air like that! Had his luck run out? Would this be the time that his life really would end?

Landon looked up and his eyes met the horse's eyes and at that moment, at that very moment… Magic backed up and plopped his hooves down onto the ground. As if a sudden burst of compassion had brought him back to reality and he realized that he was about to attack his best friend.  Magic bowed his head as if he were apologizing and both of their lives changed. Landon stood up trembling and scared. He quickly thought to himself, "is your life worth trying to train this horse?"

Landon brushed the hay off his clothes and kept thinking about how it would have felt if Magic had pounded his hooves into his body. Landon would not have been able to withstand that kind of hit. He paused and looked at the horse again and realized that he had decided to be friends with a *true beast*! This was perhaps the biggest animal that Landon had ever been around …up close. Why had Magic decided not to pound him at that very moment? After all, he had no reason to trust Landon, he barely even knew him. The only possible reason that Magic could have controlled his reactions was because he somehow cared about Landon. The only reason that Landon would have looked up at this towering beast above him was because he too cared about Magic. This moment they both recognized that they had begun to trust each other, and this was the truest sign of love.

When Landon realized that he was okay, his first thought was to make sure that Magic had not damaged the pen. Mrs. Martha would not appreciate him coming out to the barn and destroying her property. As Landon began to pick up a bucket, he kept a close eye on Magic as he leaned onto the rail. He appeared to be settled down, or was he just getting more energy to try and attach Landon again. Landon slowly moved the bucket back to its original spot and began to pick up the other items that Magic had knocked over. Magic stood against the rail breathing heavily. He was obviously hurt, and Landon slowly moved toward Magic – calmly, quietly, cautiously. You could tell that Magic was still nervous and timid. Landon proceeded with hesitation – that is when he recognized the aluminum can that was still attached to Magic's back hoof.

It would only be a simple removal but too much had already happened and Landon – did not want to press his luck. Slowly approaching to assure Magic that he would not hurt him. He began to gently stroke Magic's neck, then he moved down his back toward the hind leg. Landon gently picked up Magic's back hoof to remove the crushed can. Removing this can placed Landon in a special position, one that would gain Magic's loyalty…possibly forever. Landon had finally broken through and he would not defy Magic's trust…ever. A long, scary day turned into one of the best days of Landon's life.

As he walked Magic back to the quiet and secluded pasture, he just couldn't wait to see what would happen with their friendship now. Twice Magic had nearly attacked Landon but ultimately refused to hurt him. Landon recognized that Magic had every right in the world to hurt anyone because of the great level of pain that he had experienced. Landon understood how unsettled or angry that Magic could be after that lifestyle of abuse and pain. He couldn't imagine why or how anyone would ever want to hurt an animal. He often read about how animals were rescued because of abuse but had never been around one. This was his first experience being around an abused animal and it made him really sad to think about it. The key was to show Magic that hurting him was the last thing on his mind. He realized he had to prove his love to this massive beast, even if it took forever….even if it took forever!

# 10

# Restless Routines

# CHAPTER 10

Big Jimmy was sitting in the garage shining his shoes when Landon hopped through the back door. Big Jimmy always took pride in keeping things nice and clean – his shoes were no exception. “Little boy – you going back to that barn again?” “Aren’t you tired of that barn?” Landon’s mom asked. Mrs. Alice stood in the garage sweeping around. She shook her head at the thought of him running back and forth to that barn. “Don’t you have some other work that you can be doing? “Nope,” he mumbled as he whizzed past, “I love it even when I have to go by myself and my friends don’t show up.” “what about breakf…”? It was too late, Landon had already sped out toward the barn.

He was so anxious to get to the pasture that he actually skipped breakfast, his favorite meal! Bursting through the screen door, Landon hopped onto his bike which seemed to already be waiting for him. He pedaled through the scratchy briars that hung from the bushes as he made his way down the narrow path toward the pasture. He didn’t care if they were

bruising his arms – he had somewhere to go. When Landon arrived, he saw Mrs. Martha doing her daily chores. He glanced out toward the pasture and realized that Magic was nowhere to be seen. “Mrs. Martha, Magic is not in his favorite spot by the willow tree…where is he?” Mrs. Martha said, “Believe it or not Landon, Magic is already in the training pen, something tremendous must have happened between the two of you yesterday". Landon spun around and couldn't believe his eyes!! Magic was already inside the pen – almost as if he had been waiting on him. Soon Magic was following Landon and was listening to his every command. It was as if they had been friend's their entire lives. Landon knew that Magic had somehow loved the training pen at one point of his life, or he wouldn't have been so willing to go back into it. Landon proceeded to the tack room to find ropes to begin training him. He would be lunging Magic around and around the pen. The walking and running would help with control. Then, Landon noticed the old wooden table that sat in the corner of the training pen. He thought to himself, *maybe I can use this table to set the saddle and pad on. Once Magic gets used to seeing them sitting there on the table, he'll realize that they won't harm him.*

After lunging Magic for a short time, Landon brushed him down and gave him a treat. Landon knew that every day would just get better and better. He could see the dusk start to set in and Landon knew that it was time to head home. He decided to leave Magic in the training pen for the night. It seemed like the place he wanted to be. This warmed Landon's heart because he knew that his friend was not only willing to work hard at being trained but he was just as eager as Landon was to prove that he was ready for his first ride.

After many days of training, Landon could tell that Magic was getting restless with the routines. One particular morning when Landon arrived, he was surprised by what he saw…. hoofprints buried in the sand and the saddle and pad had been dragged away from the old wooden table. It was a mystery that had finally unfolded - lonely frustration had taken over and Magic was insisting... *"when will I get my turn?"* Landon could tell that he needed to try different methods of training with Magic in order to keep him interested and engaged. While he was trying these different methods, his parents showed up. He was surprised to see them there. When Mrs. Alice was around things were cool but to see Landon's Dad, Big Jimmy, things were serious. "Hey, what are you guys doing here?" he inquired. Mrs. Alice said, "Remember we leave for our family vacation tomorrow and your dad and I just stopped by to tell Mrs. Martha how thankful we are for her help with the youth and that you wouldn't be back for a few days". Landon stopped in his tracks and thought, "*was it time to visit the beach already?*". Landon had been so busy working and thinking about Magic that the weeks had slipped away. Landon grasped Magic's neck and squeezed him. Big Jimmy asked, "Is that Magic the horse that ran the field all alone? Wow he's beautiful". Landon replied, "Yes he is and he's my best friend. Can he come along with us on the family vacation?". Big Jimmy knew the feeling that Landon had for the horse, but he knew to leave these kinds of decisions for Mrs. Alice to tackle. Mrs. Alice had no problem saying no... and going about her merry way. Big Jimmy had a soft spot for animals and knew it would be hard to say no to Landon's request. Besides, the place they were staying had a beautiful open field right by the beach.

Surprisingly, Mrs. Alice had given a different answer – She said, " I would love for your friend Magic to come along, but we didn't make arrangements for a horse. Maybe next year we can search for an area that is horse friendly and Magic will feel right at home." While the conversation at the barn had lasted longer than usual. The sun slowly, slithered away and it was too late for Landon to ride his bicycle home. Landon stumbled into the back seat of Mrs. Alice's Jeep with his head hung over and his arms folded. He thought, "How can I see Magic one last time before I leave?". With everyone having mixed feelings the short ride home was quiet. Mrs. Alice gave an answer about Magic that was hopeful – yet it didn't solve the problem of leaving Magic behind. Big Jimmy knew the hurt that Landon was feeling, and he wanted to say, *just let the horse come along*. However, he always let Mrs. Alice make the final call. Landon wandered into the house, he didn't feel like eating, but instead plopped down onto his bed and before long, he wandered off to sleep.

# 11

# Broken

# CHAPTER 11

Family vacation day was finally here! Landon was not as excited as he thought he would be, instead he was heartbroken that he had to leave his horse. Big Jimmy was awake packing for the trip and could sense that Landon was not being himself. He walked across the hall to see if he could stir his son from sleep. Before Big Jimmy could get to the door, it slowly crept open and Landon appeared fully dressed. His faced looked tired, as if he had tossed and turned all night. Big Jimmy shook his head, "You look awful!! Is there anything that could make you feel better than you do right now? Would seeing Magic one more time help?" At that moment, Landon perked up and a wide grin appeared on his face. "Are you serious? Yes, that would definitely make me feel better!" Big Jimmy said, 'I'll meet you at the truck!"

The short ride to the barn took forever. Landon was hoping to see Magic standing in the field. Instead, there was no sign of him. Landon ran through the barn to the other side. Magic was already in the pen…waiting for his trainer and friend. This was a sad day; he had just started building their friendship and now he was going away. Landon had thought of the right words to say, he had even brought an apple treat. He led Magic from the pen to the Willow tree. Landon whispered into Magic's ear, "I must leave you for a little while but when I get back – I promise I'll never leave you again." Landon and Magic walked across the grassy field, when suddenly Magic came to a stop. He made a loud neigh and Landon could only hope that Magic was saying, "I'll be fine, but I will be expecting you every day when you return." Magic was released and he ran toward the Willow tree. After leaving, Landon sat quietly in the car all the way back home. This was going to be a rough vacation.

The first day without Landon proved to be tough. Mrs. Martha was looking out of her office window and she realized that Magic really missed Landon because he was pacing back and forth. He acted like a volcano ready to erupt. The speckled rooster scratching around shouting out loud crows was the only entertainment in the barnyard. Suddenly, Magic's head bounced up and down as if he thought he heard a familiar voice through the pines that divided the land. He walked closer to the edge of

the fence and rubbed his body along the rotten wood. Within seconds, "crack" the wood broke, and Magic was free!!

With no intentions of escape, Magic soon realized that the sounds had led him to a part of the field that he was not familiar with. Magic stopped to nibble on grass, but it was barely enough to satisfy his hunger. He looked down at the hoof hoping to find his way back, but there were too many directions for him to trace. The tired and frightened stallion wandered from field to field. Sunlight was disappearing and he needed a break. He could smell the fresh water that flowed behind an abandoned house and he felt that maybe this would be the perfect spot to stand for the night and perhaps find his way back in the morning.

As morning arrived, Magic set out again looking for more grass to munch. Soon Magic was spotted by Myla, Landon's friend from the gym. Myla yelled to her Pops, "Hey Chief, look, it's Magic - he must be lost!" Myla asked Chief to take her to the barn to alert Mrs. Martha that Magic was free. When they arrived and informed Mrs. Martha, she panicked, "Oh NO! I must get some apple treats to lure him back and keep him calm until Landon returns." Mrs. Martha hurried off to gather up some treats from her old friend, Mrs. Rose.

Chief heard the conversation between Myla and Mrs.

Martha and after Mrs. Martha left, he asked, "Are you talking about Landon the kid who plays at the children's home?" Myla replied, "Yes Chief, I promise you Landon can catch Magic". Chief thought that the horse was too big for a kid like Landon to control, much less catch. "I think it would be safer to call animal control", Chief said. He knew that an animal this size should not be running free! "NO!!" yelped Myla, "please don't, I've watched Landon over and over work with Magic he can handle that horse." Chief responded, "Well, we will give Landon until morning to come and catch this horse but if not, we will have to make the call!" Myla froze, she knew there was no way Landon would be there by morning and she needed a plan that would keep Chief distracted from making the dreaded call. Besides, he had no idea how much work Landon had already invested in helping Magic overcome his fears.

Meanwhile, Magic was still wandering around the fields unsure of which direction would lead him back to his favorite spot – the Willow tree. He wasn't sure how he had gotten this far away from his safety and needed to see familiar ground. Somehow, Magic could feel the tension around him and knew that his freedom may come to an end. If Chief had his way, Magic's destiny was going to change... perhaps forever.

# The Dreadful Call

# CHAPTER 12

Morning peeked through Myla's window. She jumped up, tossed on her clothes, and raced down the sidewalk. Within minutes, she had made it to the barn. She ran straight to Mrs. Martha's office… tired and out of breath. Myla panted, "You must understand animal control is on its way to find Magic and take him away." Mrs. Martha stood there in total disbelief. I looked everywhere yesterday and could not find him. I was hoping that he would wander back to the Willow tree. Mrs. Martha felt terrible, she had promised Landon that Magic would be safe. How was she going to tell Landon that Magic had been taken away?

Mrs. Martha was now a nervous wreck. She needed to find Magic before animal control could. She hopped into her car; she had never driven so fast! Up ahead, she could see a crowd of people gathered in a field. She pulled her car into an empty spot. She flung her door open and hobbled across the field yelling, "Stop, stop, please don't take Magic, he's on his way back to the barn". She could see Magic dashing back and forth across the land, drenched in sweat. Mrs. Martha knew he was in distress. She could tell that he was growing tired and animal control would eventually rope him and pull him onto the trailer.

Mrs. Martha yelled, “I’m the owner, just catch him and I’ll walk him to the barn.” The animal control officer approached Mrs. Martha and said, “It’s not that easy, he seems kind of wild to me.” Mrs. Martha assured him that she would be fine. She also knew that Magic was very distrusting and may not let anyone near him…except, Landon of course. How would she convince animal control that she could handle a horse with such temperament?

Back at the barn, Myla’s tears continued to fall. How was she going to tell Landon that her Dad had called animal control to come and capture his best friend? Myla sat at Mrs. Martha’s desk and looked out into the field where Magic used to run. She reached for some tissue on Mrs. Martha’s desk when she noticed Landon’s notepad. There was his contact number big as day…should she call him or let the officer capture Magic? The only chance Magic had was for Myla to contact Landon. She picked up Mrs. Martha’s phone and prepared to deliver the dreadful message. Myla gathered her words and took a deep breath to calm down before dialing the number. Big

Jimmy answered the phone. He could hear breathing in the background but no words. He knew something was wrong, he could sense it. Finally, Myla blurted out, "Magic has broken free and needs your help and Landon is the only one who can save him, you've got to come back now!"

Landon's mom, who overheard the conversation, chimed in, "We can't leave our vacation!" Jimmy responded, "Well, we will just have to plan another one – I need to try and save my son's horse. He can't be out there roaming around free. What if they don't find him, what if something horrible happens to him?" Big Jimmy returned to the call, "Myla, we're leaving now, thanks for letting us know!" Big Jimmy slammed down the phone and spun around only to see Landon sitting speechless with tears rolling down his cheeks. Big Jimmy tried to assure his son that everything would be fine. Jimmy always had a warm spot in his heart for animals and saving Magic was the only thing on his mind. As for Mrs. Alice, seeing her son in so much pain and sadness made her soften her heart. They all jumped into the truck and headed home. Big Jimmy made this journey many times and he knew that this was going to be a long ride. At the same time, he wanted to show Landon the true meaning of friendship – even if your best friend was an

animal! He knew that being there for Magic would make all the difference in the world.

As they arrived in town, traffic became congested. They patiently waited to get through the traffic. Landon watched every passing car – perhaps this would get his mind off worrying about Magic, but nothing seemed to calm his nerves. All he could think about was – *What is Magic doing at this moment?*

Back at the field, the area had been taped off and Magic was growing tired. Magic's muscles started to shrink, and his strength began to weaken. Mrs. Martha stayed right there by Magic's side trying to distract animal control as much as she could until Landon arrived. She wanted to yell to Magic, "Don't give up!" The horse trailer backed up slowly into the taped off area. The animal control officer stepped down from the truck – that is when Mrs. Martha recognized that the man was Officer Justice. Everyone in the neighborhood knew him as the one officer who was strictly by the book. There was no chance that he would wait until Landon got there. He walked around to the side of his truck and retrieved his favorite rope. As he walked towards Magic, Mrs. Martha could tell that Magic had no strength left to fight. He started backing up to a

nearby tree. Officer Justice twirled his rope around a few times and launched it up into the air. The rope landed right around Magic's neck. You could tell that Officer Justice had practiced this a lot – he did it perfectly. While being pulled to the horse trailer, Magic was dripping sweat. The look of defeat covered Magic's face and it appeared that all was now lost.

# 13

# Stop Him

# CHAPTER 13

Big Jimmy and his family finally made it through the traffic. Landon blurted out and pointed to the top of the hill, "I see a horse trailer, Magic must be there!" Mrs. Alice noticed the horse trailer too. She had a sinking feeling that they would be too late. She looked at Big Jimmy and whispered, "step on it". Big Jimmy picked up his speed. Mrs. Alice, tried to stay focused, "Calm down Landon, please!" When they reached the taped area, Landon leaped from the back seat. "He must still be here – I see his prints!" Landon yelled Magic's name, he heard nothing – there was no sign of his horse. Landon noticed Mrs. Martha at the corner of the taped off area. He knew that something was terribly wrong. "Why are you crying Mrs. Martha? Magic will come when he hears my voice, just watch." Landon turned and yelled several more times, "Magic, where are you? It's me, I'm here now!" Mrs. Martha said to Landon, "I made you a promise that I'd keep Magic safe. If I could have distracted Officer Justice just a little while longer, Magic would be here now, but there was nothing I could do."

Landon screamed, “What do you mean, what do you mean, I’m here now, why would they take him if I was coming back?” Mrs. Martha felt the tears pour down her face, “I know Landon, I watched you do amazing things with Magic and now sadly I must tell you that I watched as they hauled him away.”

Landon told Mrs. Martha, “He is your horse, why would they take him? Besides, you knew I was on my way back to get him – why didn’t you stop them?” Mrs. Alice stepped in and grabbed Landon’s shoulder and told him to calm down, “Mrs. Martha did all that she could do but she didn’t have a trailer to haul Magic off in and Officer Justice was only doing his job!” Landon paused for a moment as horror covered his face, did you say – Officer Justice? “Oh NO!! not Officer Justice, he isn’t fair. All of the animals missing now are somehow tied to Officer Justice. Magic is a special animal and Officer Justice would never take him to the right shelter”. Landon began sobbing loudly.  Big Jimmy said, “Landon, calm down and relax. Tomorrow, we’ll call and get this figured out!”

Landon stumbled to the truck, almost in shock. Mrs. Martha assured him that she would be up at the crack of dawn trying to get this all straightened out. Landon hardly slept at all that night. All he could think about was where Magic was and how he was feeling. Landon knew that he had to find Magic as soon as possible.

Somehow, he must have dozed off because when he opened his eyes, he was still lying on his bed fully dressed. He called his friends, told them what happened and ask them to meet him at the gym so they could all search for Magic. He drifted into the kitchen and Mrs. Alice said, "I hope you feel better this morning, do you want breakfast?" Landon shook his head, "No thanks, I just want to get to the gym to meet my friends. We are going to find Magic!"

When Landon arrived at the gym, no one was there. He wondered, am I going to have to do this alone? Then suddenly the door opened,

Lamar and Myla rushed in, "We're here, …let's go!" Caleb burst through the gym doors with some news. "Landon, I noticed that just before dark last night, Officer Justice was hauling a horse trailer down Williams Lane." Myla asked, "Williams Lane? That's not the driveway for the shelter!" Landon yelled out, "Let's go, we've got to find Magic." Caleb calmed the group down and said, "First, let's ride our bikes to my house. I think that there is a trail that runs behind the old creek that will get us over to Williams Lane quicker. Then we can see what is going on over there. They all jumped on their bikes and headed to Caleb's house.

After arriving at Caleb's house, they huddled together to come up with a plan. Lamar told Myla, "You look on the

left side of Williams Lane and we'll look on the right side of Williams Lane ... Okay?" Myla asked, "Look for what, Lamar?" "We're looking for the horse of course" smirked Lamar, "I thought you knew that already". Landon said, "Yeah, but who would have a pasture area down Williams Lane? Caleb said, "It sounds crazy, but I'm telling you guys I know I saw Officer Justice turn down the road pulling a horse trailer. Yes, there are lots of fancy houses there, but I know what I saw."

Caleb suddenly pointed down toward the corner house. "I told you guys that I wasn't crazy! That driveway looks like it goes around to the back of the house and that trailer is still sticking out – can you see it?" Landon stretched his neck and said, "Yea, I think I see the back of the trailer". "Caleb you were really looking, I would have never spotted that", Myla said. Lamar responded, "Yea, I see the trailer, but I don't see Officer Justice, what do you want to do Landon?" "Maybe this is just one of his family members and he stopped here to visit", Landon said. "Let's just hang out by this tree and see who comes out."

# Trapped Inside

# CHAPTER 14

After a few minutes, the front door of the house flung open and a tall man wandered out.  Myla frantically whispered, "I know him, that's Johnny Boy. He's a horse trader. He could afford a pasture down here! He's done business with my dad, Chief. I don't really like him because he trades animals all day. If he gets Magic, you may never see him again." Landon said, "Do you think Officer Justice is trying to sell my horse, would he really do something that horrible?"

Suddenly, Officer Justice appeared from around the side of the trailer. *What was he doing here talking to Johnny Boy?* Johnny Boy looked into the trailer and nodded his head. He reached for his wallet and handed Officer Justice a wad of money. The two men shook hands. "Landon, you'd better think quick, this doesn't look good," said Myla, "Maybe Magic is in the trailer."  Landon squirmed from a belly position to his knees. Officer Justice opened one side of the trailer door and the horse began to back up. "Hey, that's not Magic!" Landon whispered. There was a huge sigh of relief. But this still didn't answer the question, "Where is Magic?"

Johnny Boy walked the horse to the other side of his yard toward the open pasture. Officer Justice climbed into his truck, "Looks like a storm is coming – I have one more stop to make – gotta' get this wild stallion to where it belongs – so I'd better head out – good doing business with you Johnny - enjoy your new horse". Caleb whispered, "Did you guys hear that? I bet Magic is the wild stallion he's talking about still on that trailer!" Officer Justice backed the trailer up, barely missing the tree in the front yard. He was definitely in a hurry.

The kids bounced up from the ground and headed for the trailer. Caleb yelled, "Let's do it!!" Landon, Caleb, Lamar and Myla rushed to grab the back door of the trailer and slid into the open bay. The trailer moved so fast that they were not able to stand up.

They hopped on just in time! Landon exclaimed, "He's got to slow this thing down, I can't see anything!" Myla yelled, "I'm going to be sick!"" No time for that," shouted Caleb," just stay down low – don't try to stand up". The trailer bounced back and forth for about 10 minutes then came to a screeching halt, catapulting the kids to the other end of the single sided bay. Landon whispered, "Are you guys okay? Myla nodded her head but looked like she was frightened to death. "Shh, keep

it quiet," encouraged Caleb, "We have no idea what's going to happen." No sooner than Caleb finished his sentence, Officer Justice flung the other side of the trailer door open. Landon placed his finger up to his mouth to warn the others not to say a word. "Come on Magic, I believe that's your name, we've got some business to handle," Officer Justice chuckled.

The trailer was sitting in what appeared to be a dark tunnel, people talking and laughing. Other horses could be heard in the distance. Landon raised his brows as if to silently ask, "Where are we?" The others just shook their heads. Landon whispered, "Could this be the auction that Mrs. Martha is always skeptical about? Maybe this is why she was so suspicious of Officer Justice from the beginning". Caleb said, "It could be, but first things first, how the heck are we going to get out of this trailer without anyone spotting us?" Landon said, "I'll check and see what is going on" Landon poked his head out of the trailer and was startled by the security guard who was coming around the side of the wall. "Hey, hey what are you kids doing here…no kids are allowed at this auction - scram!! Myla yelled, "Did you hear that? He's going to put us in one of those dirty old horse stalls if we don't get out of here!!" Caleb, Lamar, Landon and Myla made a fast break from the back of the trailer and headed towards the open gate. The security guard flipped his hands - "Darn kids!!" As they bolted across the field, Landon heard a familiar sound .... he slowed down and listened. He heard a grunting sound... the sound of a sad horse..." Wait a minute you guys......it's Magic...I hear him... I can't leave now!" Caleb yelled, "Are you crazy? We can't stay here!" It was too late, Landon had already turned and headed back towards the gray, tin building. They looked at each other in disbelief. Lamar said, "Well, we can't leave Landon, we all need to stay together, so come on!" They rushed toward the building trying to catch Landon. Landon stopped outside the door. "There are people inside, we need to wait." he whispered. Once it got quiet, they opened the rusty door and tiptoed in. Once inside, they heard a startling voice, "So you kids just couldn't leave! Now, I'm going to have to place you inside this barn until I call each of your parents!!" It was the security guard and he wasn't kidding this time. He hustled them into a hay-filled room and demanded that they sit down and write each of their parent's names and numbers on the piece of paper that he shoved into their hands. They all looked at each other in disbelief.... Why did they let Landon lead them back here?

At that moment, the security guard received a radio call telling him that he was needed immediately at the far end of the auction lot. He demanded that the kids sit there until he returned, or they would be in even deeper trouble. He hurried through the narrow passageway and scooted onto his four-wheeler as he whizzed across the field.

# 15

# I Can’t Leave

# CHAPTER 15

Whew, that was close", admitted Caleb. "But we still don't know where Magic is or what we are going to do if we find him." Suddenly, they heard a loud "Thunk". "What was that?" Lamar asked. "Keep quiet someone may hear us!" They all turned their eyes towards the once open door – which was now…closed!! They peered through the slot on the side panel of the door. Apparently when the security guard left… he left the barn door open and a gust of wind had traveled inside and slammed the door closed. Myla wiggled the doorknob and started screaming, "We're locked inside, we're locked inside!!" "Calm down!" shouted Caleb, "I need to think for a second, don't panic!!" Caleb took a deep breath… "Let's not give up so easily. There has got to be a way to get out of here!!We just need to think." Landon said, "Let's look around and see if there is anything that we can use to pick the lock open." Myla shouted, "Do you know anything about picking a lock open, this isn't television, we're trapped in here!!" At that moment, Lamar spotted a set of keys hanging on the side of

the fence pole and yelled, “Look - keys…but they’re too far to reach!” That is when Caleb saw a fallen hay rake on the ground near the door. There was enough space under the door that a rake might just fit through. He bent down and stretched his thin arm under the stall door. He wiggled his fingers as if to stretch them a bit longer but…. nothing. “I can’t quite get it”, he muttered! “Let me try,” Landon demanded. He laid down on his belly and stretched out as far as he could, but nothing… then, out of no where..he had a flash of his horse in his thoughts and it seemed that his arm grew another 2 inches… just enough to grab the corner of the rake .“I got it, he yelled!” Landon dragged the rake to the edge of the door and bent it upward. Just enough to pull it through the small opening. “Yes!! You did it Landon!” shouted Myla.

Once the rake was inside of the stall, Landon handed it to Caleb. “Your turn”, he said. Caleb grabbed the rake and gently shimmied it toward the keys on the metal hook. He knew he had maybe one shot at getting the keys or they would be stuck until the security guard got back and perhaps brought Officer Justice. They could not wait until then. They had to get out of the stall before the guard got back. Caleb stretched the rake across the alley way to gently lift the keys

MISSING

off the post. Everyone was holding their breath and within a few seconds the keys were hooked on the wooden rake. The kids screamed to the top of their lungs, “Yes! We did it”. No time to waste, let’s figure out which key it is and let’s get out of here. They tried two keys and the third one was success. They flung the door open and Landon rushed into command mode, “Myla – you get in the office and call Mrs. Martha – tell her what’s going on; she will know what to do. Caleb come with me and we will try to find Magic… hopefully it won’t be too late!! Lamar, you keep a watch out for the security guard and Officer Justice.” The kids raced to their assigned positions but also realizing that they needed to stay out of sight. As Myla dashed off to the office, she knocked a large container down off the corner shelf. Papers flew everywhere! She stopped to grab them but saw that they were posters…. all with pictures of lost or missing horses!! “Wait you guys look at this!” Landon said, “We don’t have time to stop, we have got to get Magic. “No, you need to see this”, she demanded. Caleb and Landon looked at each other and turned to go back to Myla. They couldn’t believe what they were looking at dozens of reported...lost or missing horses. Could Officer Justice be running an illegal horse ring? Were all the horses here trapped like Magic? There was only one way to find out and they were not going to stop until they had answers. “Come on Caleb, grab those pictures, we have to save some horses!” Landon shouted.

Myla looked around the room and couldn’t spot a phone anywhere, then suddenly she noticed an old phone hanging on the wall. Myla thought to herself, “There is no way that old phone still works”. Myla picked it up and couldn’t believe that she heard a dial tone. She remembered that her grandmother had a phone like this a long time ago. Myla remembered her using her finger to turn the numbers. She tried that and surprisingly, it worked! She quickly dialed Mrs. Martha who happened to be sitting at her office desk doing her own investigation of Officer Justice. “Mrs. Martha,” Myla gasped, “you’ve got to help us, we are at the barn there are horses they have been missing, the boys are trying to free them now.” “Whoa, slow down” yelped Mrs. Martha. “I can’t understand a word you are saying!” “Okay, give me a minute” requested Myla. “We’re trapped at the old auction barn – down by the bridge at the end of town, please save us.” Mrs. Martha knew exactly where the call had been made from. She remembered that old auction barn from when she was a young girl. “I know where you guys are – hold tight!” As Mrs. Martha made her way out of her office, she decided to call the police for backup because she didn't know what to expect once she showed up at the auction lot.

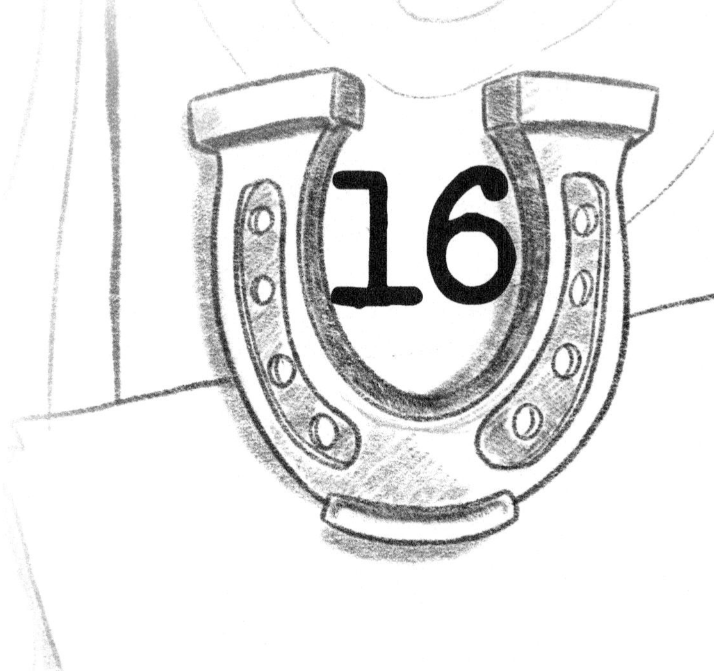

# 16

# Don't Do It

# CHAPTER 16

Meanwhile, Caleb and Landon arrived at the worn-down wooden building. They hurried inside and crouched under a table. This would be the safest place to hide until they could figure out what was going on. They began to recognize that all the horses on the posters they were holding, were horses inside of the building. Landon saw every horse from the flyers, but Magic was nowhere to be seen. This was definitely an underground horse ring!! Caleb and Landon couldn't believe that these innocent animals had been held hostage by these horrible horse traders. People had been looking for these animals for so long. They had no choice but to help free these animals. Landon scooted from under the table and tiptoed to the first gate to free the beautiful variety of horses. From paint horses to quarter horses, they were all beautiful and majestic. When he turned to look at Caleb to inform him that he had unlocked the gate, the corner of the gate flew from his fingers and flung against a tin wall making a horrendous sound. The loud sound not only scared Landon but it also spooked the horses. They all began to scatter. Landon barely moved out of the way in time.

At that moment, Officer Justice ran in from around the corner holding his rope in his hand. He wasn't sure what to do at that moment – horses were running everywhere. Then he spotted the kids, "Wait a minute – what's going on…what are you kids doing in here?" he shouted. Caleb and Landon froze in their tracks. Officer Justice moved closer to them, almost forgetting about the horses. He twirled his rope into the air as if he were about to strike Landon. "You're a thief" Landon shouted! "You've got to be stopped!" Officer Justice turned as red as a beet - and yelled, "You're not taking my prize horses, nobody is!!" "Magic belongs to me", Landon yelled. Magic suddenly appeared from the crowd of horses and headed toward Landon at full speed. As Landon plowed toward Magic – he grabbed him around his neck and hoisted himself onto the horse. This was the first true ride of their friendship… and it was going to be a wild one! Magic raced around in the barn with Landon hanging on. He almost knocked Officer Justice to his feet, but he managed to keep his balance while still twirling the rope. It was clear that Magic was looking for the nearest escape route. Officer Justice turned around and around twirling his rope hoping to land another perfect lasso. As Officer Justice lost control of his rope, it started to slip from his hands falling to the ground. Still spinning in circles, the rope tangled around Officer Justice's feet and he stumbled and hit the ground hard. This unexpected motion spooked Magic causing him to lunge forward with great force. Landon couldn't hold on any longer and he felt himself catapult forward. His knees burrowed into the dirt and Magic cantered towards Officer Justice! Officer Justice struggled to get back onto his feet, but Magic circled him with a quick pace then Magic lifted his front hooves high above Officer Justice's head. Magic stretched them out far and began grasping at the air. Landon screamed out, "Don't Magic – Don't do it! Whoa!" Then within a few inches – Magic planted his hooves onto the ground barely missing Officer Justice's skull. Magic took one hard blow as if to say, "This was your lucky day". Magic backed up and waited for his next command. At that moment, Landon whistled for Magic to come closer. Magic roamed toward Landon as if he expected the huge hug that Landon was about to give him. Magic laid his neck onto Landon's shoulder and their friendship had been sealed. Landon turned to look at Officer Justice –who he raised his head, looked at Magic, then placed his face back down into the ground. He too realized that this had been his lucky day!

Mrs. Martha burst through the wooden building - roaring like a lion but as mad as a rattlesnake. Sirens could be heard in the distance. She yelled, “Officer Justice, I knew you were up to something all this time!!”– She leaned over him with her hands on her hips, “You hear that?– those sirens are for you - How dare you treat these animals this way and how dare you even think about harming these kids! Your days of injustice are coming to an end .... today!” Officer Justice slowly pulled himself up into a sitting position. He knew that when the police arrived, he would have a lot of explaining to do. The police engulfed the wooden building – and quickly apprehended Officer Justice. Then they yelled, "Okay everyone, we're here - you're safe" After the kids heard the police officer's voices they emerged from their hiding places. Caleb and Lamar came from under the desk. Myla peeped from behind the curtain. They knew they were safe, and the mystery of the missing horses could now be solved – but Officer Justice needed to tell the whole truth about what happened. Horses had been missing in this town for months and no one could really explain what was going on, now everything was starting to make sense. Caleb shook his head and asked, "What are we going to do with all of these horses – what now?" The officers said, "These are some beautiful horses and we definitely need to move them, but we have no place to board them until we find their rightful owner."

# 17

# Never Again

# CHAPTER 17

Mrs. Martha went into operation horse mode. She told the kids to round the horses up and try to get them into the corral located at the back of the auction building. She then told the officers that her barn would be the ideal location until the owners were contacted. "That's a great idea," Landon shrieked as he rushed through the barn door with Magic right on his heels. "Did you say surround the scattered horses?" he asked. "That's a job for Magic and me." Magic bellowed out a loud Nay sound in agreeance. Landon jumped onto Magic with an incredible ease. This was going to be a much better ride. Landon rode out and began to circle the horses until they were all corralled together and ready to be moved away. While the officers were lining up the trailers and getting ready to board the horses one by one, Big Jimmy and Mrs. Alice arrived. They had heard about Officer Justice and the illegal auction and they also came prepared with an empty trailer. After Landon and Magic finished rounding up the horses, Landon walked Magic onto his own trailer and grasped him around the neck and whispered, “We are back together, and I promise to never leave you again”. Mrs. Martha suggested, “Maybe after we get the horses transported, unloaded and settled into the barn we can have a big celebration while everyone is still together.” Mrs. Alice smiled and said, “That sounds like a great plan, but we have one stop to make first!” Landon was curious as he leaned over the front seat to see what his mom was talking about. “Back into your seat belt young man... you’ll know soon enough.” Big Jimmy gently pulled into the gravel driveway so as not to disturb Magic. This horse had already been through enough. Mrs. Rose was digging in her flowers as always. She looked up and spotted the trio pulling the trailer. She slipped off her red rubber glove and waved it into the air. Mrs. Alice opened the truck door and hopped out, “Hello Mrs. Rose, we know it has been a while, but would you happen to have more apples that we could grab? We just saved some horses from Officer Justice and we thought that would keep them calm until we find their owners. Mrs. Rose paused for a moment and wiped the sweat from her brow. “Of course, anything for the horses – but no one has been in the backyard since Landon. If there are any left, they are yours”. “Excuse me, did you say, 1 Officer Justice with animal control? I knew there was something sneaky about him, but no one ever listened. I never trusted him much." The trio looked at each other in shock. How did everyone see that except them?

Landon raced around to the back of the truck and grabbed his blue bucket and headed for the apple tree. "Hey wait up", yelled Mrs. Alice. "I want to help too!" As they were filling the bucket, you could hear the thump, thump until the bucket was full of delicious treats. Landon could hardly lift the bucket. "Big Jim to the rescue," chuckled his dad as he hoisted the bucket up like it only weighed a few pounds.

“Do you mind if I ride along? asked Mrs. Rose. She was never really one who got excited about leaving home, but this time she was eager to join the crowd. “Why sure!” Mrs. Alice replied,” you took the words right out of my mouth – without you, we wouldn’t have these yummy treats to give those poor, scared horses!” Do you have a ladder? I’ve never gotten into a truck this big!!” They all laughed in unison. “Take your time Mrs. Rose,” encouraged Mrs. Alice. Once she had climbed safely inside – they took off towards Mrs. Martha’s barn where all the other horses were waiting to be reclaimed. Big Jimmy didn’t seem to be driving fast enough for Landon. “Dad, why are you driving so slow!!?” “Safety first son, safety first – it won’t be much longer, Big Jim assured. “I actually like his pace,” chimed Mrs. Rose – “this is just my speed – steady but sure!” They arrived at the barn and everyone seemed to be adjusting well. Caleb, Lamar and Myla were unloading and moving horses around. Greyson came running toward Landon. “Friends, friends where have you been!!??” yelled Greyson. “I haven’t seen you guys in 100 million years!!” Landon, Myla, Lamar and Caleb all smiled and gave Greyson lots of high fives and hugs. He was the one who always gave Landon encouraging words and reminded him to never give up on the wild stallion that he fell in love with. Greyson looked up the hill and pointed to the gym. "When are we all going back to our meeting place? he asked. It was true, Landon had gotten so caught up in the horse and training, vacation and auctions and thieves, that he had literally forgotten about the gym. He had even dragged all his friends into helping him. For the first time since all of this happened, Landon realized that he had missed the playing, fussing and maybe even the fights over basketball. "I know buddy, but this is another way for all of us to connect as a family – helping these horses had to be done." "Can I help?" asked Greyson. "Sure", smiled Landon, "just hand me that blue bucket of apples over there." Landon looked at the others and started snickering, they knew that the bucket was too heavy and just wanted to tease Greyson. "Just kidding buddy" laughed Landon, "we'll all do it together!!" The kids were having so much fun that they didn't realize that the sun had slowly faded away. The horses were comfortable and relaxed, feeling right at home.

# Celebration

# CHAPTER 18

The scent from the delicious, prepared food was sailing through the air. Mrs. Rose who turned out to have a funny sense of humor spoke up, “Who prepared the food? It really smells good, but you know I don’t eat everybody’s cooking. The horses shouldn’t be the only thing around here with a full stomach.” Mrs. Alice raised her hand and smiled, “No worries, I’m the cook”. Mrs. Rose nodded her head and said, “Gee Whiz, I’ve heard so much about your food and finally I’m able to taste it for myself. So, play some music, bring out the food and LET’S EAT!” Big Jimmy, Landon, Caleb, and Greyson rose up from their seats and walked into the room that held all of the delicious food. They grabbed pans, one at a time, and prepared the table. Big Jimmy chuckled, “I’m out of breath – I must be getting old!!” Landon blurted out, “This sure is a lot of food!!” After a few minutes Landon shouted, “The food is ready!” Greyson yelled, “I’ll say the blessing”. After the blessing, everyone grabbed their plates and headed towards the incredible mound of food. Utensils clinking together was the only noise that could be heard in the joyous barn. Suddenly, Mrs. Martha stopped and tilted her head towards the open barn door.

She heard a truck creeping up the gravel driveway. "Who could that be?" she wondered as she peeped through the barn window. Barely able to see, Mrs. Martha spotted a tall man approaching the barn. She stood off to the side waiting until she could get a clearer glimpse. She quickly noticed that it was Chief, Myla's dad. Opening the door to welcome him, she exclaimed, "Well, Hello Chief, come on in and join us – we just started eating" Myla looked up and the expression on her face revealed shock. She said, "Hello Dad, what brings you here?" Chief replied, "Well, the sun has gone down and riding a bike home just doesn't seem safe. So, I'd feel better picking you up." Chief paused and was astonished at how everyone had come together over stolen horses. You could see that he was troubled about something. He finally spoke up and admitted, "I remember that I tried to ruin Landon by separating him from his magnificent stallion. If I could only forget the past but since I can't, I'd like to at least apologize. Also, if Mrs. Martha would agree to it, I would love to transform her barn into a boarding facility for rescued horses. The horses could get the love and care they need to live a better life. Even the homeless horses can have a forever home." "Are you serious, Dad? You would really do that for us, if Mrs. Martha agrees?" yelled Myla. "Sure, I owe that to you all. That is the very least I can do," said Chief. They all turned to Mrs. Martha. "Well, what do you think, would you do this for the horses?" Mrs. Martha started to cry and said, "Anything for the kids and the animals – I love them all so much!" At that moment, everyone started jumping up and down and hugging each other – this had really turned into a REAL celebration. Everyone started thanking Chief for his generosity and the joy that they all felt about being together. As it got later, they knew it was time to leave. Caleb spoke up, “Wait everyone, before you leave, now that we have established a great relationship with horses maybe now we can build our friendships back in the gym”. After all, that is what our summer was supposed to be about anyway…spending time at the gym! Greyson cheered, “That is a great idea!” Landon smiled back and replied, “Well, I guess I will see you guys tomorrow on the hill, at the gym!!” Everyone started to load up in their cars to leave and Landon pleaded, “Wait mama and daddy – I’ve got one more thing to do!” Landon raced out the back door and back down toward the barn. Alice looked at Big Jimmy and just shook her head. Landon could see Magic’s neck sticking through the open stall segment and he ran and grabbed him. “Magic, I know all of our days together have not been fun. Most of them have been frustrating and frightening. Still somehow, we made it back together again. You saved our lives and if only you understood the words that I am speaking to you…I just want to say thanks! Even forgiving Officer Justice, giving him a second chance… saying I love you is still not enough.” Suddenly, Magic turned his head down and placed it across Landon's shoulders as if to say, "I understand everything you are saying friend and I love you back". Landon could feel his eyes well up and knew that it was time to go. He turned around to head out the door and heard Magic let out a soft Nay, as if to say goodnight. When Landon got outside, he thought about how he was so worried that his summer may be boring and long. It was hard to believe that there were only a few more weeks before school would start again. He had made closer friends, nearly trained a horse and help bust horse thieves! This was far from a boring summer. He smiled to himself and jumped into the car. Alice and Big Jimmy turned around to him. "I'm proud of you Landon", said Mrs. Alice, "Me too", chimed in Big Jimmy. "Now, let's get you home - you've got a busy day tomorrow!" Landon slid down into the back seat and wondered what his next day would be like with his friend. He closed his eyes and drifted off to sleep thinking about the incredible summer that he had encountered and the new life ahead for Magic and him.

Made in the USA
Columbia, SC
21 July 2021